This daily journal is dedicated to YOU, a young
dreamer and creator. Take each day as a chance
to learn, experience new things, and improve
the world.

We believe in you!

GET IN TOUCH

hello@biglifejournal.com

LEARN MORE

www.biglifejournal.com

Printed in Canada

Published by Eidens, Inc.
©2020 Eidens, Inc.

10 9 8 7 6 5 4 3 2 1
v1

This journal belongs to:

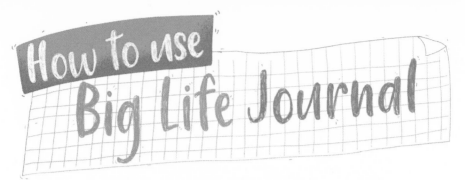

How to use Big Life Journal

This is a special journal that will help you create the mindset you need to achieve all your dreams in life!

This journal is yours, so YOU make the rules! Here's one way you can use it:

- Complete the "I Am Uniquely Me" pages first.

- Read the introduction on pages 8-13 alone or together with a grown-up (in case you have any questions).

- Begin your daily journal! Choose a time each day when you want to write in your journal—for example, after dinner or before bedtime. It's totally fine to skip some days, too!

Remember, each time you write in your journal, your brain gets a boost of confidence, gratitude, and positivity!

WHAT'S INSIDE

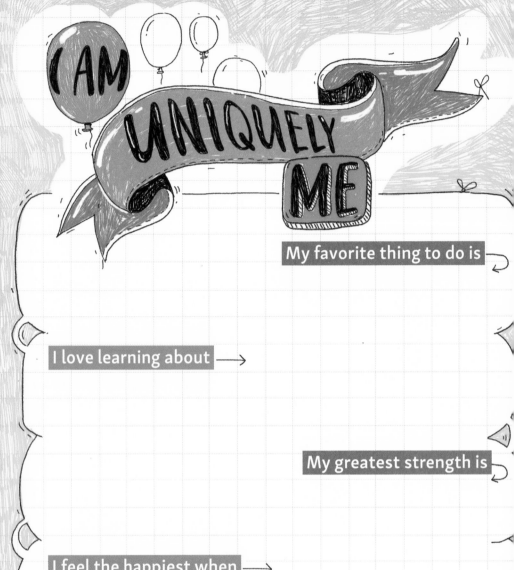

I AM UNIQUELY ME

My favorite thing to do is

I love learning about →

My greatest strength is

I feel the happiest when →

I would like to get better at

6

If I opened a store,
I would sell...

If I wrote a book,
it would be about...

If I could build anything,
I would build...

If I could go anywhere,
I would go to...

1

YOUR BRAIN IS YOUR SUPERPOWER

Your brain helps you learn new things and get better at stuff... so that you can do cool, awesome things in life!

How? Every time you LEARN something new or figure HARD THINGS out, your brain creates new cells. And when you PRACTICE, your brain builds new connections between its cells.

The activities and things you're learning become EASY for you because your brain grows and changes!

Write down the activities that were once hard for you and then became much easier with practice. Think about activities like riding a bike, counting, reading, roller-skating, playing an instrument, or drawing.

 Failure makes you
strong and resilient.

 Failure helps you learn
what doesn't work.

 Failure builds
your character.

 Failure helps you learn
how to solve problems.

 Every failure is a stepping
stone to success.

WHEN I FEEL UPSET, WORRIED, OR DISAPPOINTED, I CAN...

Visualize a peaceful place

Play with modeling clay

Listen to relaxing music

Draw how I feel

Write in a journal

Look at my

glitter jar

Go outside

Jump on a trampoline

Stretch

Make a fist,

then relax

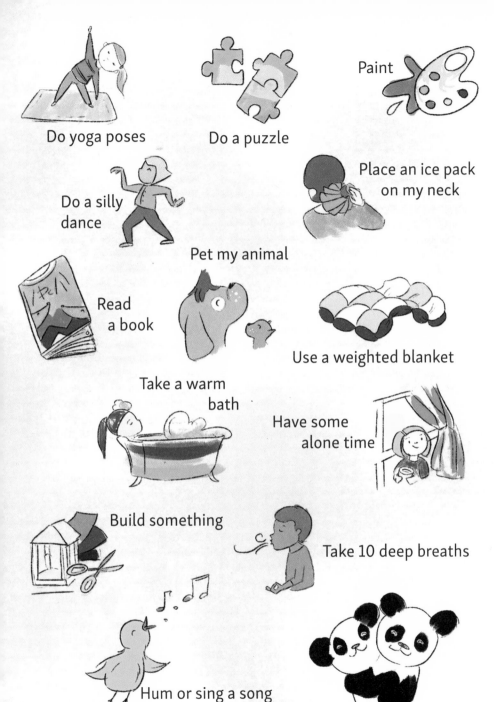

Do yoga poses

Do a puzzle

Paint

Do a silly dance

Place an ice pack on my neck

Pet my animal

Read a book

Use a weighted blanket

Take a warm bath

Have some alone time

Build something

Take 10 deep breaths

Hum or sing a song

Give someone a hug

Date: _____

Today I learned:

Today I felt (circle more than one face if you'd like):

I'm not sure if they will like my new hat.

If YOU like your new hat, that's all that matters!

Value what YOU think of yourself more than what other people think of you!

Date: _____

Today I am grateful for:

Today I felt:

You can draw your own face here

The best part of my day (draw or write about it):

Date: _____

One great thing that happened today:

Today I felt:

How I made a difference for someone recently
(draw or write about it):

Date: _____

Something that made me laugh today:

Today I felt:

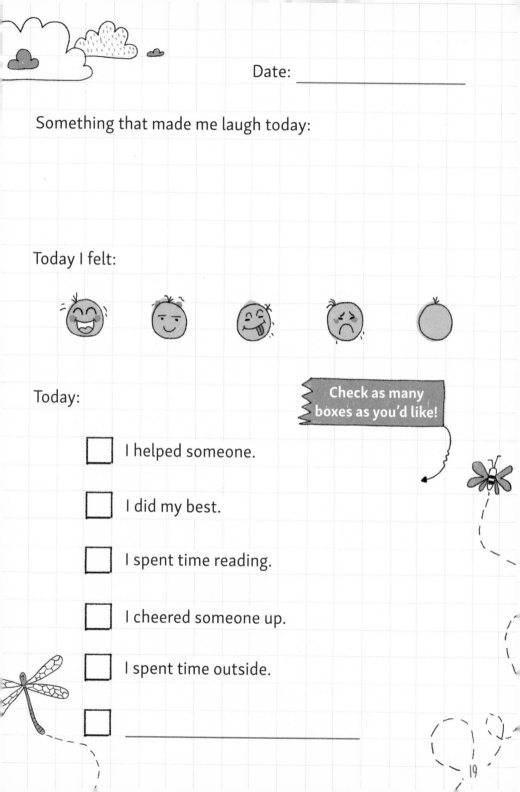

Today:

Check as many boxes as you'd like!

☐ I helped someone.

☐ I did my best.

☐ I spent time reading.

☐ I cheered someone up.

☐ I spent time outside.

☐ _____

Date: _____

Today I learned:

Today I felt:

Sometimes we just need to try a different way of doing
something. Think of something hard you're learning.
What's something new you could try?

Date: _____

Today I am grateful for:

Today I felt:

The best part of my day (draw or write about it):

Date: _____

One thing I love about myself:

Today I felt:

Something hard I accomplished recently
(draw or write about it):

Date: _____

One great thing that happened today:

Today I felt:

Today:

☐ I did something kind.

☐ I was brave.

☐ I made a mistake and learned from it.

☐ I learned something new.

☐ I had fun.

☐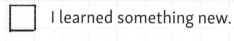

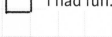

23

Date: _____

Today I learned:

Today I felt:

Think of something you want to learn, do, or become.
This will be your GOAL! Use page 112 to break down
your goal into small steps you can take each day.

Date: _____

Today I am proud of myself for:

Today I felt:

Something that didn't go as planned today
(describe what happened):

Next time, I will:

Date: _____

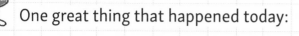

One great thing that happened today:

Today I felt:

How I made a difference in someone's life recently (draw or write about it):

Date: _____

Something that made me laugh today:

Today I felt:

Today:

☐ I asked lots of questions.

☐ I gave hugs to someone I love.

☐ I practiced something I am learning.

☐ I met someone new.

☐ I played a fun game.

☐ _____

Date: _____

Today I learned:

Today I felt:

In every situation, focus on the things you can control:
your actions, your words, your attitude, and your choices.

Date: _____

Today I am grateful for:

Today I felt:

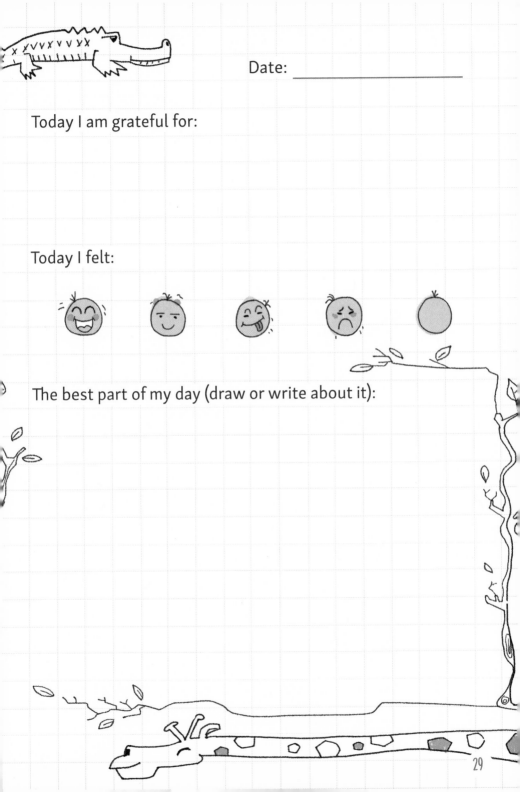

The best part of my day (draw or write about it):

Date: _____

One thing I love about myself:

Today I felt:

Something hard I accomplished recently
(draw or write about it):

Date: _____

One great thing that happened today:

Today I felt:

Today:

☐ I was curious.

☐ I solved a problem.

☐ I worked on something hard.

☐ I asked someone for help.

☐ I slept well.

☐ _____

Date: _____

Today I learned:

Today I felt:

I feel sad and bored.

It's okay to feel that way sometimes.

We have so many feelings throughout the day:
happiness, boredom, anger, fear, and many others.
It's all just part of being human!

Date: _____

Today I am proud of myself for:

Today I felt:

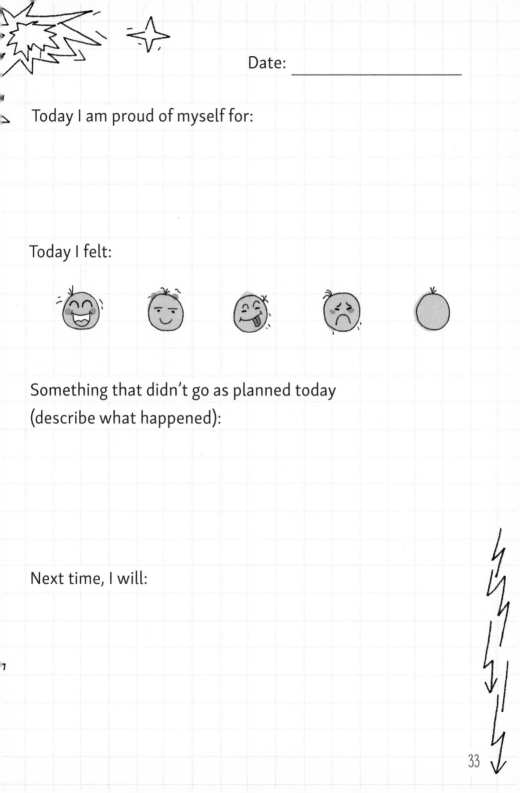

Something that didn't go as planned today
(describe what happened):

Next time, I will:

Date: _____

One great thing that happened today:

Today I felt:

How I made a difference in someone's life recently
(draw or write about it):

Date: _____

Something that made me laugh today:

Today I felt:

Today:

☐ I was creative.

☐ I felt proud of myself.

☐ I played together with someone.

☐ I ate a healthy meal.

☐ I found a way to feel better when I got upset.

☐ _____

Date: _____

Today I learned:

Today I felt:

What are you doing?

I'm thinking about things I couldn't do before that I can do now. It makes me feel brave.

Use page 113 to list things you can already do. Look at this list whenever you want to feel a little braver and stronger.

Today I am grateful for:

Today I felt:

The best part of my day (draw or write about it):

Date: _____

One thing I love about myself:

Today I felt:

Something hard I accomplished recently
(draw or write about it):

Date: _____

One great thing that happened today:

Today I felt:

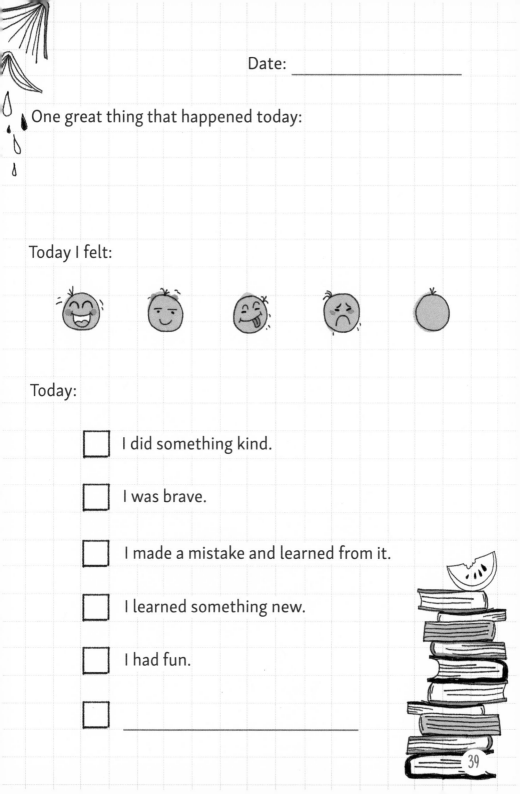

Today:

☐ I did something kind.

☐ I was brave.

☐ I made a mistake and learned from it.

☐ I learned something new.

☐ I had fun.

☐ _____

Date: _____

Today I learned:

Today I felt:

Practice makes progress! What is something you want
to begin doing? Set aside some time to
practice it regularly (every day or every week).

Date: _____

Today I am proud of myself for:

Today I felt:

Something that didn't go as planned today
(describe what happened):

Next time, I will:

One great thing that happened today:

Today I felt:

How I made a difference in someone's life recently
(draw or write about it):

Date: _____

Something that made me laugh today:

Today I felt:

Today:

☐ I helped someone.

☐ I did my best.

☐ I cheered someone up.

☐ I spent time reading.

☐ I spent time outside.

☐ _____

Today I learned:

Today I felt:

I think I made a mistake.

We all make mistakes when we're learning! They help our brains grow!

When you learn from your mistakes, you help your brain grow! Think of one mistake you made recently. What did you learn from it?

Date: _____

Today I am grateful for:

Today I felt:

The best part of my day (draw or write about it):

45

Date: _____

One thing I love about myself:

Today I felt:

Something difficult I accomplished recently
(draw or write about it):

Date: _____

One great thing that happened today:

Today I felt:

Today:

☐ I asked lots of questions.

☐ I gave hugs to someone I love.

☐ I practiced something I am learning.

☐ I met someone new.

☐ I played a fun game.

☐ _____
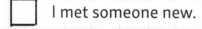

Date: _____

Today I learned:

Today I felt:

There will always be someone better or worse than you at things, but that doesn't matter one bit. Focus on your own progress and how you improve over time!

Date: _____

Today I am proud of myself for:

Today I felt:

Something that didn't go as planned today
(describe what happened):

Next time, I will:

49

Date: _____

One great thing that happened today:

Today I felt:

How I made a difference for someone recently
(draw or write about it):

Date: _____

Something that made me laugh today:

Today I felt:

Today:

☐ I was curious.

☐ I solved a problem.

☐ I worked on something hard.

☐ I asked someone for help.

☐ I slept well.

☐ _____

Date: _____

Today I learned:

Today I felt:

I entered my poem into a competition, but they said, "No."

That just means you are one step closer to your next "YES."

Rejections are a part of life! You can look at each "no"
as a learning opportunity to improve and try again!

Date: _____

Today I am grateful for:

Today I felt:

The best part of my day (draw or write about it):

Date: _____

One thing I love about myself:

Today I felt:

Something hard I accomplished recently
(draw or write about it):

Date: _____

One great thing that happened today:

Today I felt:

Today:

☐ I was creative.

☐ I felt proud of myself.

☐ I played together with someone.

☐ I ate a healthy meal.

☐ I found a way to feel better when I got upset.

☐ _____

Date: _____

Today I learned:

Today I felt:

What is one thing you don't like about yourself?

Hmm...nothing. I love and accept myself just the way I am!

Being loving and kind to yourself is very important. When you love yourself, you feel strong, brave, and unstoppable!

Date: _____

Today I am proud of myself for:

Today I felt:

Something that didn't go as planned today
(describe what happened):

Next time, I will:

One great thing that happened today:

Today I felt:

How I made a difference for someone recently
(draw or write about it):

Date: _____

Something that made me laugh today:

Today I felt:

Today:

☐ I helped someone.

☐ I did my best.

☐ I cheered someone up.

☐ I spent time reading.

☐ I spent time outside.

☐ _____

59

Date: _____

Today I learned:

Today I felt:

Why are you so happy today?

When I woke up this morning, I decided it was going to be a great day!

You can CHOOSE to have a good day by saying,
"Today will be great!" as soon as you wake up.
Continue to look for positive things throughout the day.

Date: _____

Today I am grateful for:

Today I felt:

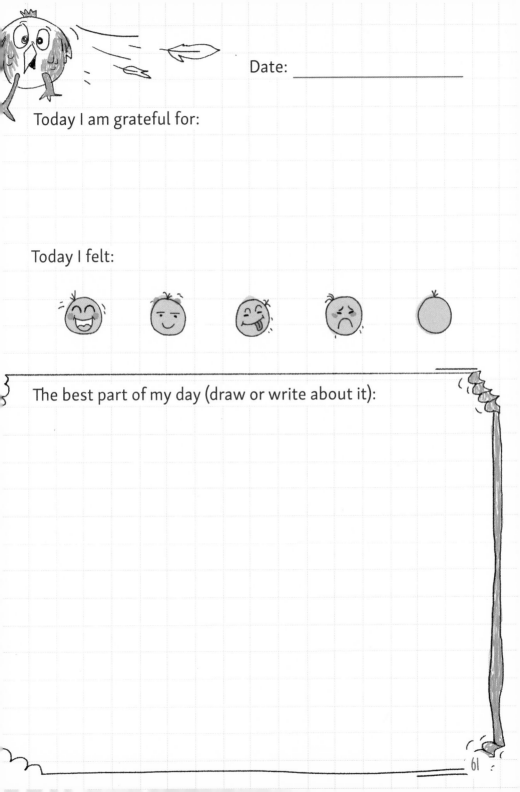

The best part of my day (draw or write about it):

Date: _____

One thing I love about myself:

Today I felt:

Something hard I accomplished recently
(draw or write about it):

Date: _____

One great thing that happened today:

Today I felt:

Today:

☐ I did something kind.

☐ I was brave.

☐ I made a mistake and learned from it.

☐ I learned something new.

☐ I had fun.

☐ _____

Date: _____

Something I learned today:

Today I felt:

Before asking others if they like your work, think about how it felt for you to create it. Remember that the most important thing is how YOU feel about your work.

Date: _____

Today I am proud of myself for:

Today I felt:

Something that didn't go as planned today
(describe what happened):

Next time, I will:

Date: _____

One great thing that happened today:

Today I felt:

How I made a difference for someone recently
(draw or write about it):

Date: _____

Something that made me laugh today:

Today I felt:

Today:

☐ I asked lots of questions.

☐ I gave hugs to someone I love.

☐ I practiced something I am learning.

☐ I met someone new.

☐ I played a fun game.

☐ _____

Date: _____

Today I learned:

Today I felt:

How's it going?

I can't do it YET!
But I'm getting better
each time I try.

Use page 114 to make a list of things you can't do YET
but want to learn. Sometimes we just need to give our
brains and bodies more time to learn new things!

Date: _____

Today I am grateful for:

Today I felt:

The best part of my day (draw or write about it):

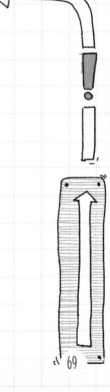

Date: _____

One thing I love about myself:

Today I felt:

Something hard I accomplished recently
(draw or write about it):

Date: _____

One great thing that happened today:

Today I felt:

Today:

☐ I was curious.

☐ I solved a problem.

☐ I worked on something hard.

☐ I asked someone for help.

☐ I slept well.

☐ _____

71

Date: _____

Today I learned:

Today I felt:

Asking for help is a great strategy when you feel stuck.
Think of something you're struggling with.
Whom can you ask for help?

Date: _____

Today I am proud of myself for:

Today I felt:

Something that didn't go as planned today
(describe what happened):

Next time, I will:

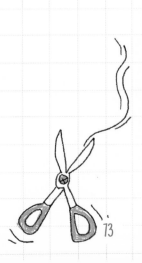

73

Date: _____

One great thing that happened today:

Today I felt:

How I made a difference for someone recently
(draw or write about it):

Date: _____

Something that made me laugh today:

Today I felt:

Today:

☐ I was creative.

☐ I felt proud of myself.

☐ I played together with someone.

☐ I ate a healthy meal.

☐ I found a way to feel better when I got upset.

☐ _____

Date: _____

Today I learned:

Today I felt:

I wish all things were easy.

We don't grow when things are easy. We grow when we face challenges.

When we go through challenges or difficult situations, we become stronger. Think of a challenge you recently faced in your friendships, at school, or while learning something. What is one thing you learned from it?

Date: _____

Today I am grateful for:

Today I felt:

The best part of my day (draw or write about it):

Date: _____

One thing I love about myself:

Today I felt:

Something hard I accomplished recently
(draw or write about it):

Date: _____

One great thing that happened today:

Today I felt:

Today:

☐ I did something kind.

☐ I was brave.

☐ I made a mistake and learned from it.

☐ I learned something new.

☐ I had fun.

☐ _____

Date: _____

Today I learned:

Today I felt:

Is there anyone you know who is struggling with something or feeling sad? How can you share your kindness with that person?

Date: _____

Today I am proud of myself for:

Today I felt:

Something that didn't go as planned today
(describe what happened):

Next time, I will:

Date: _____

One great thing that happened today:

Today I felt:

How I made a difference for someone recently
(draw or write about it):

Date: _____

Something that made me laugh today:

Today I felt:

Today:

☐ I helped someone.

☐ I did my best.

☐ I cheered someone up.

☐ I spent time reading.

☐ I spent time outside.

☐ _____

Date: _____

Today I learned:

Today I felt:

I'm trying hard, but I can't make it perfect.

What matters is that you do your best.

Making something perfect is not the goal.
The goal is doing your best with what you have.

Date: _____

Today I am grateful for:

Today I felt:

The best part of my day (draw or write about it):

Date: _____

One thing I love about myself:

Today I felt:

Something hard I accomplished recently
(draw or write about it):

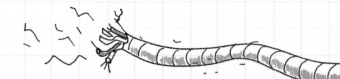

Date: _____

One great thing that happened today:

Today I felt:

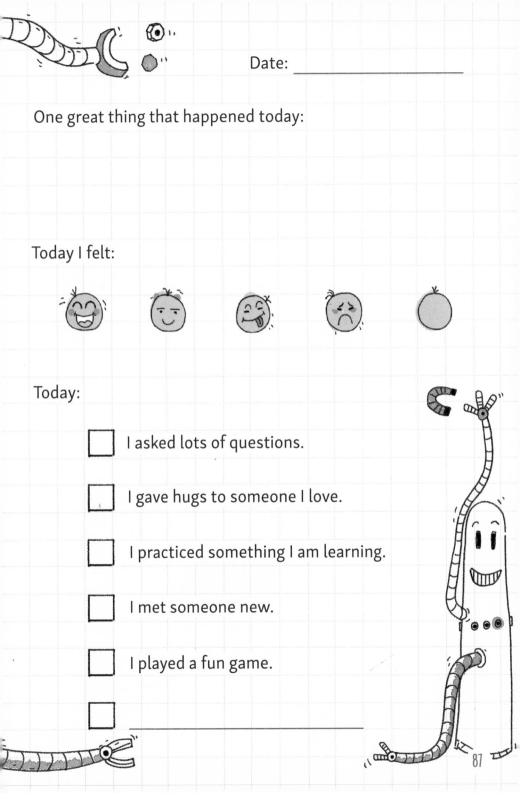

Today:

☐ I asked lots of questions.

☐ I gave hugs to someone I love.

☐ I practiced something I am learning.

☐ I met someone new.

☐ I played a fun game.

☐ _____

Date: _____

Today I learned:

Today I felt:

Grades and achievements matter, but learning is always
the most important thing. Ask an adult to help you understand
how you can use what you're learning, today and in the future.

Date: _____

Today I am proud of myself for:

Today I felt:

Something that didn't go as planned today
(describe what happened):

Next time, I will:

Date: _____

One great thing that happened today:

Today I felt:

How I made a difference for someone recently
(draw or write about it):

Date: _____

Something that made me laugh today:

Today I felt:

Today:

☐ I was curious.

☐ I solved a problem.

☐ I worked on something hard.

☐ I asked someone for help.

☐ I slept well.

☐ _____

Date: _____

Today I learned:

Today I felt:

I don't like going places where I don't know anyone.

I understand, and it's okay to feel that way. You can be scared and do it anyway!

Trying new things and meeting new people can be uncomfortable at first. Think of a time when you tried something that was scary at first but so much fun in the end.

Date: _____

Today I am grateful for:

Today I felt:

The best part of my day (draw or write about it):

93

Date: _____

One thing I love about myself:

Today I felt:

Something hard I accomplished recently
(draw or write about it):

Date: _____

One great thing that happened today:

Today I felt:

Today:

☐ I was creative.

☐ I felt proud of myself.

☐ I played together with someone.

☐ I ate a healthy meal.

☐ I found a way to feel better when I got upset.

☐ _____

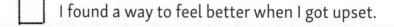

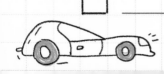 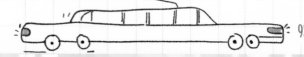

95

Date: _____

Today I learned:

Today I felt:

When you remember all the things you're grateful for, you become happier, healthier, and stronger. Go to page 115 to list things you're grateful to have, do, and be.

Date: _____

Today I am proud of myself for:

Today I felt:

Something that didn't go as planned today
(describe what happened):

Next time, I will:

Date: _____

One great thing that happened today:

Today I felt:

How I made a difference for someone recently
(draw or write about it):

Date: _____

Something that made me laugh today:

Today I felt:

Today:

☐ I helped someone.

☐ I did my best.

☐ I cheered someone up.

☐ I spent time reading.

☐ I spent time outside.

☐ _____

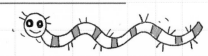

Today I learned:

Today I felt:

Learning something fast isn't always the best way to learn. When you take your time to learn something, you understand it better.

Date: _____

Today I am grateful for:

Today I felt:

The best part of my day (draw or write about it):

Date: _____

One thing I love about myself:

Today I felt:

Something hard I accomplished recently
(draw or write about it):

Date: _____

One great thing that happened today:

Today I felt:

Today:

☐ I did something kind.

☐ I was brave.

☐ I made a mistake and learned from it.

☐ I learned something new.

☐ I had fun.

☐ _____

103

Date: _____

Today I learned:

Today I felt:

You've been doing this for so long, but you haven't given up.

I believe I can do it! And that helps me to keep going.

Believing in yourself means trusting yourself to achieve anything, asking for help when you need it, and doing your absolute best. What is something you believe you can learn or achieve in the future?

Date: _____

Today I am proud of myself for:

Today I felt:

Something that didn't go as planned today
(describe what happened):

Next time, I will:

105

One great thing that happened today:

Today I felt:

How I made a difference for someone recently
(draw or write about it):

Date: _____

Something that made me laugh today:

Today I felt:

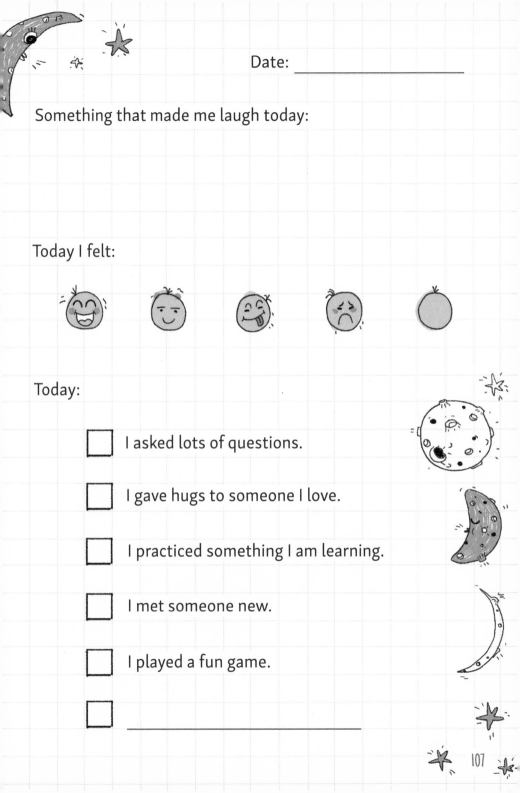

Today:

☐ I asked lots of questions.

☐ I gave hugs to someone I love.

☐ I practiced something I am learning.

☐ I met someone new.

☐ I played a fun game.

☐ _____

Today I learned:

Today I felt:

Sometimes you might be worried if others will like you.
Remember that your true friends will always accept you
as you are!

Date: _____

Today I am grateful for:

Today I felt:

The best part of my day (draw or write about it):

Date: _____

One thing I love about myself:

Today I felt:

Something hard I accomplished recently
(draw or write about it):

Date: _____

One great thing that happened today:

Today I felt:

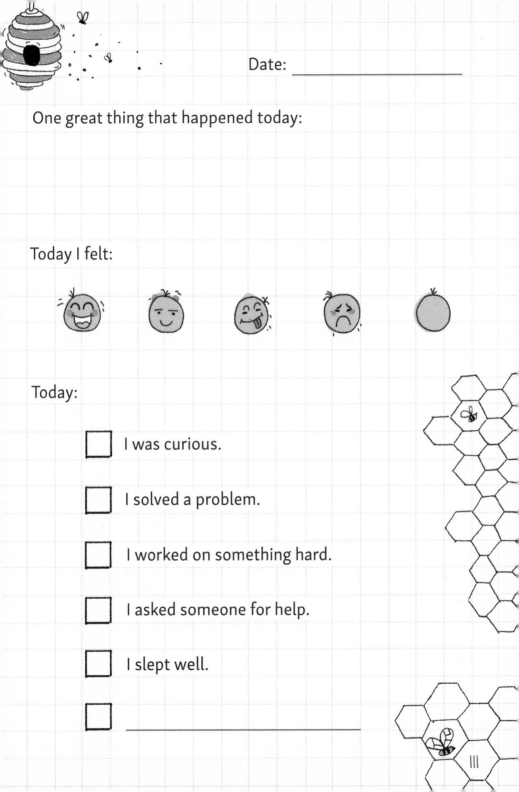

Today:

☐ I was curious.

☐ I solved a problem.

☐ I worked on something hard.

☐ I asked someone for help.

☐ I slept well.

☐ _____

MY GOAL

Something I want to learn, do, or become:

I want to achieve my goal by (date):

Things I can do to work toward my goal:
(Examples: practice once a week, read a book on the topic, talk to an expert)

People who can help me if things get difficult:

Things I Can Already Do

Things I Can't Do YET

...and Want to Learn!

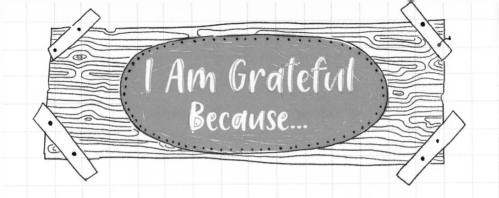

I Am Grateful Because...

I am

_____

I can

_____

I have

_____

Get the original **Big Life Journal** with interesting stories and fun activities!

You will discover:
- how to believe in yourself
- how mistakes help you learn and grow
- how you can achieve anything when you're persistent

"My favorite part of Big Life Journal is the stories. The journal teaches me to never give up."
- Thalo, age 7

Great for ages 7-10

the BIG LIFE KIDS PODCAST

Two best friends, Zara and Leo, are flying their magical vehicle, Believemobile, around the world to tell stories of remarkable people who chase their dreams and never give up!

"I really like the podcast. I've learned so much!
It gives me a confident mindset!
I've been listening every day."
- Emerson, age 6

Go to biglifejournal.com/podcast to listen!

Always Believe You Can!

As you finish your *Big Life Journal*, remember that you can do, be, and learn anything you want!

You have the power to make all your wildest and biggest dreams come true! There's no limit to how far you can go.

No challenge is stronger than you are. You have everything you need to overcome any obstacle, and you're never alone.

The world is a beautiful place. You have unique abilities, an amazing imagination, and ideas to make it even better. The world needs YOU!

Always believe you are strong and capable.
Always believe you can!

Alexandra Eidens
Author and Cofounder of *Big Life Journal*

Written by **Alexandra Eidens**.

Design and illustrations by **Emilia Jesenska** and **Aleksandra Korableva**. Cover by **Tania June** and **Emilia Jesenska**.

Special thanks to **Dr. Carol Dweck** for her body of work on growth mindset theory.